DUTCH PAINTING

DUTCH PAINTING

FROUKJE HOEKSTRA

PARK
LANE

Cover illustrations

- Johannes Vermeer
  The Painter's Studio, 1665-70 (detail)
  Vienna, Kunsthistorisches Museum
- Willem van de Velde
  The IJ at Amsterdam, 1686
  Amsterdam, Rijksmuseum

First published in Great Britain in 1994
by Grange Books PLC
The Grange, Grange Yard, London SE1 3AG

This edition produced in co-operation with Arcturus Publishing Ltd.

Translated from the Dutch by Tony Langham and Plym Peters

Coordination and production: VBI/Smeets, Weert
Filmset: Zspiegel grafische zetterij, Best, The Netherlands
Print: Royal Smeets Offset b.v., Weert, The Netherlands

© Royal Smeets Offset b.v., Weert, The Netherlands

ISBN 1 85627 692 9

DUTCH PAINTING

The great age of painting in the Netherlands started at the end of the fourteenth century with the so-called Flemish Primitives, and lasted for more than three centuries until the end of the Golden Century.

The whole area, which was divided towards the end of 1500 into the Northern and Southern Netherlands, produced an unbelievable amount of talent for that period of three hundred years, including some men of absolute genius such as Jan van Eyck, Rogier van der Weyden, Hieronymus Bosch, Pieter Bruegel, Rubens, Frans Hals, Rembrandt and Vermeer.

This edition contains a short survey of the development and influence of painting in the Northern Netherlands, later the Republic of the Seven United Netherlands.

The Flemish were the leading painters in the Netherlands for two centuries, after which their role was largely taken over by Dutch painters in the seventeenth century. This was the start of the Golden Century of Dutch painting, which was characterized by a hitherto unheard of multiplicity of masters, styles and genres, of which the most important are covered here with examples.

Hendrik Goltzius
Portrait of Giovanni Bologna
Drawing in chalk, 37 x 30 cm
Haarlem, Teylers Museum

THE NETHERLANDS

The development of painting in the Netherlands is closely linked to the economic power of the various different areas in the Low Countries. Painting first flourished in Flanders, which was under the dominion of the powerful and art-loving dukes of Burgundy at the end of the fourteenth century. Many Flemish artists worked at the Court of Burgundy at Dijon, but the Limburg brothers from Nijmegen, who produced the incomparable book of hours, *Les Très Riches Heures du Duc de Berry*, in 1413-1416, were also there. This is a masterwork in the International Gothic style which was developed by Flemish painters. Jan van Eyck (c. 1390-1441), who was born near Maastricht, the painter who perfected the technique of painting in oils and developed an entirely new style, was the court painter in Dijon (Philip the Good) and of the Count of Holland. Van Eyck stayed at the court in The Hague for two years and had a great influence on early painting in the Northern Netherlands. In fact, very little remains of this early, mainly religious art from the Northern Netherlands, because of the wave of Iconoclasm which swept the Netherlands in 1566.

The prosperous district of Flanders, with its main cities Bruges, Ghent and Ypres, developed in the fifteenth century to become the most important artistic centre of Europe next to Italy. It was particularly in that century that Flemish art influenced the art of other countries, especially the surrounding countries, Germany and France. During this period the influence even spread to Spain. By the end of the century, the art of the Italian Renaissance became the great example for the whole of Europe, and continued to be so until the age of Rubens and Rembrandt.

Towards the end of the fifteenth century, the Southern Netherlands, and later the Northern Netherlands, fell under the power of the Hapsburgs, and Charles V united the entire area in the first half of the sixteenth century to create the seventeen Provinces of the Netherlands. It was during this period that Protestantism was introduced into the Netherlands. In 1517, Luther published his 95 Theses, and his ideas spread rapidly through northern Europe, although he was excommunicated in 1521 and Charles V started the Inquisition in 1522.

At the beginning of the sixteenth century, Antwerp became the most important port in Flanders because Bruges was cut off from the sea when the port was silted up. Antwerp grew steadily to become the greatest trading centre in Europe and also became one of the most important centres for art and culture. During its heyday, the Painters' Guild of Antwerp had more than three hundred masters, and the international climate of the city attracted many intellectuals, including writers and humanists. However, the great golden age of this Catholic port lasted a relatively short time.

In many parts of the Netherlands the opposition to the persecution of Protestants (mainly Lutherans and Calvinists) by the Catholic government soon became very strong. This persecution became even more cruel when the Spanish Inquisition was introduced during the reign of Philip II, who succeeded Charles V in 1555. Thousands of "heretics", including many intellectuals, fled from Flanders, and particularly from Antwerp to the Northern Netherlands, where opposition to the Spanish reign developed into a revolt which led to the Eighty Years' War in 1568. Admittedly the Southern Netherlands remained under Spanish dominion, but there was great unrest. The wave of Iconoclasm started in southern Flanders in 1566 and spread across the entire Netherlands. Countless churches and abbeys were pillaged and destroyed, and the prosperous cities such as Antwerp suffered particularly heavy losses. Ten years later, Antwerp was ruined in the Spanish Fury. The Spanish mutineers rampaged through the city, looting and setting fire to everything in their way. There were thousands of victims. For a time, the Southern Netherlands joined the north in the fight against Spain, but this alliance did not last long. When Antwerp surrendered to the Spanish troops in 1585 after a lengthy siege, the river Scheldt was blockaded by the Northern Netherlands, which had actually formed an independent republic. This blockade meant the end of Antwerp as an international port, a role which was soon taken over by Amsterdam. During the

Twelve Years' Truce (1609-1621), Antwerp did recover to some extent, and once again became a centre of art, overshadowed by the figure of genius, Rubens. However, the city never regained its status as a powerful trading port. The decline of Antwerp economically and culturally not only led to the flourishing of Amsterdam, but also contributed to the growth of a number of northern cities as centres of trade and culture.

THE NORTH

Until the seventeenth century, Flanders was the great artistic centre of the Netherlands, but this is not to say that the northern Low Countries did not produce any important painters up to that time. However, there was hardly any continuous tradition of painting in the north, as there was in Flanders, which attracted many painters from the north. One of the main northern cities in the fifteenth century was Haarlem, which had an important painters' guild, and where Frans Hals became a great master two centuries later.

The most important master from Haarlem (and from the Northern Netherlands) dating from this early period was Geertgen tot Sint Jans (c. 1460-c. 1490). However, his work, which was rediscovered at the beginning of this century, is entirely overshadowed by his contemporary, Hieronymus Bosch (1450-1516), from 's-Hertogenbosch, whose visionary work has a unique place in the history of art. Hardly anything is known about Bosch's life, but in a sense he is the link between the Northern and Southern Netherlands, and can be considered as a representative of both parts. His work reveals the influence of northern painters such as Geertgen, and of southern masters such as Jan van Eyck. Bosch incorporated both these elements in his incomparable oeuvre. His horrific hellish visions and biblical scenes, often full of incomprehensible symbols, are populated by grotesque figures and fantastic monsters. His allegorical and moralizing paintings reveal a pessimistic view of mankind, which was greatly appreciated by his contemporaries, particularly in the strictly Catholic Spain. Bosch had no apprentices, but his work, which reflects a time of war, disasters and the persecution of witches, was so popular that it was endlessly copied and imitated.

For example, Pieter Bruegel (1528/30-1569) produced a lot of work in the style and spirit of Hieronymus Bosch. Bruegel was born near Breda, but this painter, who is immortalized in his scenes of Flemish peasant life, cannot be viewed as a painter from the Northern Netherlands, in view of the fact that he worked in Antwerp and Brussels all his life. However, Bruegel had a fairly strong influence on painters from the Northern Netherlands with his carefully detailed scenes from daily life.

In Bruegel's time the journey to Italy to study the work of the classical and renaissance masters had become an almost compulsory trip for young painters. However, not all artists were influenced by the great Italian examples. Bruegel made the journey, but there are hardly any echoes of this in his work, and the same applies to Pieter Aertsen (1509-1574), who came from Amsterdam, but worked in Antwerp from 1535 to 1560. In Aertsen's work the daily life of the people is the main subject, as in Bruegel's paintings. He represented this in vivid, powerful compositions which are remarkable for their naturalism and warm use of colour.

An artist who falls between the late medieval art of northern Europe and the Renaissance, is Lucas van Leyden (1489/94-1533). This painter and copper engraver was a brilliant apprentice of Cornelius Engebrechtsz. (c. 1468-1533). He worked in Leiden all his life, and in his late paintings he was strongly influenced by the Venetian school, while the German master, Albrecht Dürer (1471-1528), had a great influence on Van Leyden's engravings.

HAARLEM AND UTRECHT

A large number of artists in the Netherlands assimilated the Italian imagery they had studied in Rome so completely that they were called "Romanists". The Haarlem painter, Maerten van Heemskerck (1498-1574), was a representative of Dutch Romanism who was particularly inspired by Michelangelo. His fellow citizen, Cornelis Cornelisz. van Haarlem (1562-1638), painted mainly biblical and mythological scenes in the mannerist style. This style developed at the end of the Renaissance, and was characterized by the absence of the classical Renaissance rules, to produce more tension and expression in the representation. Another mannerist from the so-called Haarlem school was Karel van Mander (1548-1606), who has an important place in the history of art, not because of his paintings, but because of his "Schilder-Boeck" (1604), which contained biographies of artists.

Apart from Haarlem, Utrecht was the second leading centre of mannerism in the Netherlands. In Utrecht, painters were influenced by the Italian artist, Caravaggio, at the beginning of the seventeenth century. These so-called "Caravaggists" included primarily Hendrick Terbrugghen (1588-1629) and Gerard van Honthorst (1590-1656). They adopted the use of colour, the realistic visual forms, and the chiaroscuro (the use of the effects of light and dark) from the Italian master. This new style of painting was very successful and was surprising not so much because of the subject matter - biblical and secular scenes - but because of the way in which these scenes were depicted. One of the main themes was the depiction of musicians in colourful garments, such as Terbrugghen's *Flute Player* (1621). These were large half-figures who seemed to be captured in movement, with the light falling diagonally on them, producing strong contrasts. With this style of composition, and the way in which they used the effect of light and dark, the painters of the Utrecht school had a great influence on the early work of artists such as Frans Hals, Rembrandt and Vermeer.

THE GOLDEN AGE

The new styles of the schools of Haarlem and Utrecht heralded the Golden Century of Dutch painting, which produced an unbelievable variety of styles and genres. This diversity was also related to the fact that the Dutch painters were not concentrated in one city, as was the case in the Southern Netherlands, where Antwerp was the only centre of artistic activity. In the Northern Netherlands there were important groups of painters, not only in Haarlem and Utrecht, but also in Amsterdam, Delft, The Hague and Leiden, and in less central cities, such as Leeuwarden, Middelburg and Zwolle. To a greater or lesser extent, each of these cities produced an individual style and an individual preference - for example, Middelburg was the city of painters of flowers - and this significantly contributed to the overwhelming wealth of imagery of the Golden Century.

The political and economic situation in the Republic of the United Netherlands was an essential factor in these turbulent developments. Following the secession from Spain, which officially took place in 1609, although the Eighty Years' War went on until 1648, there was a period of undisturbed expansion in the north. Trade and industry flourished, and the citizens became increasingly prosperous. In the Calvinist Republic, there was religious freedom (although not everyone could express their beliefs in public). The Roman Catholic Church played only a subordinate role, and this meant the disappearance of the traditionally greatest source of commissions for artists.

The most important commissions now came from the court, the aristocracy, the government, regents, musketeers, craft guilds, and prosperous citizens. This diversity of patrons not only resulted in new genres - works of musketeers are a genre unique in Dutch painting - but also in a rapid increase in the number of painters. This was particularly related to the fact that wealthy citizens had acquired a taste for collecting paintings, and there was a mania for collecting which has never been surpassed. Citizens bought paintings as investments and as status symbols, but undoubtedly also as attractive wall decorations. Commissions from the court, the government and regents were important to the artists financially, and in terms of prestige, but the number of works arising from such commissions was insignificant in comparison with the enormous number of paintings bought by private citizens.

The Calvinist taste of the Northern Netherlands had an essential influence on the development of the various genres and themes. The baroque exuberance of Flemish painting, particularly the powerful, violent and dramatic mythological and biblical genre scenes, was not at all popular. Rembrandt was one of the few Dutch painters who still used these themes, although the religious subjects particularly were very precarious in the Republic because of their Catholic associations. There was a preference for more subdued genres, and portraits, landscapes, townscapes and still lifes were the favourite themes for the Dutch painters of the Golden Century.

THE PORTRAIT

Frans Hals (1580/85-1662), who originally came from Antwerp, but moved to Haarlem early on, where he was an apprentice of Karel van Mander, was undoubtedly one of the greatest seventeenth century portraitists. Like no other painter, Hals succeeded in capturing the impression of the moment, even in the formal works of musketeers, which are amongst his most famous paintings. In addition to works of musketeers and other group portraits, he painted countless individual portraits and so-called genre portraits (such as *The Gypsy Woman*), in which he developed a hitherto unusual number of different variations in the composition. The half figure, bust, whole figure, or three-quarter figure formed the basis of the compositions in which the movement which is captured plays an essential role. This innovative master of the art of portraiture, who dealt with all the possibilities of the theme so exhaustively that he had hardly any followers in Haarlem, used the effects of paint and light so skilfully that the works were extraordinarily expressive. Occasionally painters imitated his works slavishly, and one of the few to rise above this was Johannes Verspronck (1597-1662), who adopted Hals's subtle use of colour in his individual portraits of children.

REMBRANDT

In his later work, Hals used more muted colours, which clearly reveal the influence of Rembrandt, the greatest master of all in Dutch painting. Rembrandt van Rijn (1606-1669) was born in Leiden, where he was apprenticed to become a painter. He lived there until 1631, when he moved to Amsterdam, where he worked until his death. In 1627, Rembrandt was already receiving commissions from the Stadtholder, Frederik Hendrik, and he had the title of court painter, which contributed to the rapid growth of his prestige in Amsterdam. The artist's early work, mainly historical pieces and family portraits, was still strongly influenced by Caravaggio, whose use of the effects of light and dark had a decisive influence on Rembrandt's development as a master of chiaroscuro. In Amsterdam, Rembrandt soon gained a reputation as a portrait painter, but he was also commissioned to paint group portraits of regents and biblical scenes (for the Stadholder). He completed his most famous work, the monumental painting of musketeers, *The Nightwatch*, in 1642, the year in which his wife, Saskia, died. That year also marked the end of a prosperous period. After the highly acclaimed *Nightwatch*, Rembrandt received no more important commissions, and for the rest of his life he was pursued by financial problems, though these did not in any way impede his productivity. The dynamic, broad style of his compositions made way for a more austere and profound style in about 1650, reflecting his maturity as a painter. It is interesting to follow his development from the series of penetrating self-portraits which he painted throughout his life, and with which he has a unique place in the history of art.

The innovative genius Rembrandt, as a painter, etcher and drawer, worked in virtually every genre from portraits to landscapes, and left his mark on a whole generation of painters, including a large number who had been apprenticed to him. These apprentices included, amongst others, Gerard Dou (1613-1675), Ferdinand Bol (1616-1680), and Govert Flinck (1615-1660), who was one of the most popular painters of historical works of his time, and became the most sought-after painter from Amsterdam when his teacher fell from grace. Perhaps the most talented apprentice was Carel Fabritius (1622-1654), who died very young. He assimilated Rembrandt's influence into his own sensitive style. However, most other young painters adapted to the aristocratic, fashionable style which had already emerged in the work of Thomas de Keyser (1596/97-1667), an older contemporary of Rembrandt's, who had already developed his style before Rembrandt had reached a mature stage in his work. In this style, the emphasis is on perfect technique and an external elegance, without the dramatic tension of Rembrandt's use of light and dark. A good example is formed by the bright and technically skilled portraits and works of musketeers by Bartholomeus van der Helst (1613-1670), which were more popular with patrons than *The Nightwatch*.

LANDSCAPES

Landscapes were among the most popular subjects of private collectors, and it is probably partly because of this that the Golden Century produced an enormous number of excellent landscape painters. The most diverse sorts of landscapes were painted for the prosperous Dutch interiors: fantastic mountain panoramas, views of the Rhine, "Italian" imaginary landscapes, topographically identifiable landscapes, and realistic Dutch landscapes. It is not possible to indicate exactly when the landscape became popular as an independent genre. There was a tradition of landscapes in the painting of the Southern and Northern Netherlands, and Flemish painters had even been employed by Italian artists such as Titian, especially to paint landscapes, but until the end of the sixteenth century, it had always had a more or less subordinate place.

The Flemish painter, Joachim Patenier (1475/80-1524) is seen as the first artist who specialized in landscapes, but his imaginary landscapes always contained biblical scenes, even if they had a less prominent place in the composition than was usual at that time. Peter Bruegel also had a pronounced preference for landscapes, and he often represented the landscape in a very realistic and "pure" way in his drawings and prints. However, his paintings always contained narrative elements, such as, for example, in the idyllic and idealized landscape, *The Magpie on the Gallows*, which contains some obvious - and some less obvious - symbolic references. Even the apparently pure landscapes, the series, *The Months*, contain a narrative aspect, and are hardly ever a realistic depiction of an existing landscape. Moreover, the series of *The Months* builds on the tradition of the miniatures in the books of hours, which are the earliest examples of true landscapes depicted as accurately as possible. Landscapes were a popular subject for prints, which were all the rage in Flanders in the sixteenth century. Painters such as Bruegel produced large series of landscape prints for the internationally celebrated Antwerp art dealer and publisher, Hieronymus Cock. The distribution of these prints undoubtedly contributed to the development of landscape painting in the Northern Netherlands. Cock published many original works, though he had actually started by publishing prints made after copies of works by important masters. These anticipated our modern reproductions, which enable painters and art lovers to become acquainted with international works of art. These prints were influential, but the most important influence on Dutch landscape painting probably came from Flemish painters such as Gillis van Coninxloo, Gilles de

Hondecoeter, Roulant Savery, and David Vinckboons, who had fled to Amsterdam and Utrecht because of their religious beliefs. They were the first artists in the Republic to paint landscapes, and others soon followed their example. The fantastic "cosmic" landscapes of the Flemish artists, which incorporated all sorts of diverse elements, were one example, and even Rembrandt painted landscapes in this style, but in addition, a great diversity of types of landscapes developed. There was a significant movement towards realism, which can perhaps be partly explained by the Calvinist view that nature is a reflection of God's power, and that an understanding of nature is a way of understanding God's intentions for the world.

DUTCH LANDSCAPES

This realism in the representation of nature is found above all in Dutch landscapes. The winter landscapes by Hendrick Avercamp (1585-1634), which were influenced by Bruegel, are very early examples of this. In Avercamp's works the bustle of figures on the ice which represent all levels of society is the central element, and it is as though nature sets the scene. However, in the *View of the River in Winter* by Aert van der Neer (1604-1677), the main focus is on the wintry landscape, and the figures are assimilated in it. The cool colours mean that the viewer almost feels the cold in this extremely naturalistic painting by the Amsterdam landscape painter, who was particularly famous for his sunsets and landscapes by moonlight. *A Winter Scene* by Isaak van Ostade (1621-1649), one of the many landscape artists from Haarlem, who died at a young age, exudes a completely different atmosphere. This work is similar to the landscapes of Salomon van Ruysdael, with soft tones and figures which are in a harmonious unity with the landscape. The scene probably has a moralizing content which we can no longer discern, as was the case in many seventeenth century paintings.

The "narrative" landscapes by the Haarlem artist, Philips Wouwerman (1619-1668), such as *The White Horse*, use a sophisticated technique and subtle composition and use of light. Despite the prominent place of the beautifully painted white horse, this painting must be considered to be a landscape and not a painting of an animal. The artist was very successful in his own time because his work complied with the prevailing taste for elegant composition, light colours and technical perfection.

Typical Dutch landscapes with large expanses of sky and water are the subject of the work of Salomon van Ruysdael (1600-1670) and Jan van Goyen (1596-1656). The atmosphere, composition and use of colour in their paintings were so similar for a long time that they were sometimes confused. However, the style of Ruysdael's work changed drastically after 1640, when the colours became deeper, and the compositions were often dominated by a powerful group of trees or a wide expanse of water. The broad landscape under a vast sky of clouds was represented in a very personal style by the Amsterdam painter, Philips Koninck (1619-1688). His vast, panoramic landscapes made an important contribution to Dutch landscape painting with their surprising use of colour and wonderful balance between the sky and the land.

The Haarlem painter, Jacob Isaackz. van Ruisdael (1628/29-1682), a nephew of Salomon's, was an artist who painted mountain scenes as well as Dutch landscapes - dune landscapes and distant views of Haarlem. A journey to Germany resulted in a series of monumental paintings with a strongly romantic character, such as *Landscape with the Jewish Cemetery*. In about 1656, Jacob moved to Amsterdam, where he had a large number of apprentices. The most famous of these was Meindert Hobbema (1638-1709), who excelled in painting trees. His most original work is *The Avenue, Middelharnis*, which differs from his often rather clichéd compositions, and in which the geometry of the avenue, the trees and the land produces a striking and vivid image.

PAINTINGS OF ANIMALS

Landscapes with animals have a special place in Dutch landscape painting. Paulus Potter (1625-1654) was the main representative of this genre. In addition to his paintings of horses and his famous young bull, Potter painted numerous landscapes with animals during his short career, devoting equal attention to the animal and the landscape. A large number of painters, including Adriaen van de Velde, Aelbert Cuyp and Claes Berchem produced endless variations on this theme, though none equalled the expressive power of Potter's work. These variations also included hunting scenes (not a very popular subject in the Northern Netherlands) and paintings of poultry, in which Melchior d'Hondecoeter (1636-1695) was a supreme specialist.

SEASCAPES

In the watery Republic which expanded in the seventeenth century to become a powerful seafaring nation, not only the river landscape but also the sea was an important subject. These seascapes can be divided into two main groups: the works based on the themes of the sea and the coast, in which the aspect of the landscape is dominant, and the maritime works, in which the activity at sea - naval battles and fleets - are the real subject. The first specialist in the field of seascapes is the Haarlem painter, Hendrick Vroom (1566-1640). In 1592 he had made designs for a series of tapestries portraying the Anglo-Dutch victory over the Spanish Armada in 1588. The earliest seascapes known by him date from 1607. In these works all the attention is focused on the detailed portrayal of the ships, while the sea and the sky are represented in an almost primitive way. In his work there is not yet any hint of the representation of the atmosphere in which later Dutch landscape artists were so interested, and in which they remained unsurpassed.
The most famous Dutch painter of seascapes is undoubtedly Willem van de Velde de Jonge (1633-1707), who was the apprentice of the gifted seascape painter Simon de Vlieger (c. 1600-1652), like the Amsterdam merchant/painter, Jan van de Capelle (1626-1679). The warm light and brown tones of the groups of ships outlined against the silvery sky and clouds are characteristic of Van de Capelle's work. This atmosphere can also be found in the early work of Willem van de Velde, who started to use brighter colours later on, and then concentrated almost entirely on paintings of ships and naval battles. This was also a speciality of Willem's father, Willem van de Velde de Oude (1611-1693), who was the first to join the fleet so that he could be present at battles in order to make drawings in situ. There was a great demand for paintings of naval battles at the time of the Dutch triumphs at sea, but when the English became the great maritime power, the interest in this subject soon waned. In 1673, the Van de Veldes moved to London, where they painted the battles of the English fleet, as court painters of Charles II. The Amsterdam painter, Ludolf van Backhuysen (1631-1708), is the most important representative of the last generation of painters of seascapes. Apart from peaceful views of harbours, he painted scenes of ships in stormy weather which were full of atmosphere and extremely popular.

ARCHITECTURE

The seventeenth-century interest in the environment, and the need to represent this in a realistic way, is illustrated in the fascinating paintings of architecture. The great innovator in this field is the Haarlem artist, Pieter Jansz. Saenredam (1597-1665). He painted the interiors of churches and external facades of buildings with mathematical precision. His paintings were based on accurate preliminary drawings and a detailed observation of the angle of the light and of colour. The work of this artist, who has a unique place in Dutch painting, not only reveals a thorough knowledge of the laws of perspective, but also great skill and a good feeling for the use of light. His townscapes, such as *The Old Town Hall in Amsterdam*, are a good example of the genre which developed fully in the second half of the seventeenth century. Emmanuel de Witte (1617-1692), who worked in Delft for a long time, also worked mainly on church interiors, but in contrast with the topographically precise works of Saenredam, he often painted imaginary interiors. De Witte combined various elements in order to create scenes full of atmosphere in which the light plays on the space in a way that is typical of the Delft style.

GENRE PAINTINGS

The genre paintings - a term which was only introduced in the nineteenth century - are paintings which represent different sorts of scenes from daily life. Art historians such as B. Haak prefer to call the works which fall into this category "paintings of figures", which is a clearer title for this type of painting. The common characteristic in these paintings of figures is that they include one or more anonymous figures, i.e., no portraits and no biblical or mythological figures. Some of the subjects which were very common were groups of people enjoying themselves, scenes in the inn, musicians, soldiers and "peasants", and earlier versions of this sort of work were the paintings of Pieter Bruegel, for example. In addition, there are the paintings of burghers with scenes set in interiors which have a more intimate and subdued quality such as *The Sick Woman* by Gerard Dou (1613-1675), a member of the Precise school, who came from Leiden, or *The Letter*, by Gerard ter Borch (1617-1681), who worked in Haarlem and Deventer.

Gerard Dou, Adriaen van Ostade (1610-1685) and Jan Steen (1626-1679) were the most popular genre painters of their time. Of the three, Jan Steen was undoubtedly the most versatile, and he observed scenes in inns, festivals and carousing with as much eye for detail as scenes from domestic life. These had a moralizing undertone which often portrayed human weakness with humour. In seventeenth-century paintings even apparently wholly realistic scenes almost always have a moralizing or symbolic significance, although the need to give an extra dimension to the paintings seemed to decline towards the end of the century. The double meaning of the scene could also be at the erotic level, and a fairly clear example of this is the *Gallant Scene* by Frans van Mieris (1635-1681), in which the dogs mating in the background are an indisputable symbol of lust. These representations can also be found in the works of the Amsterdam painter, Gabriel Metsu (1629-1667), such as *The Sick Child*, which is distinct from most other genre paintings because of its warm tones and soft lines. In paintings of burghers there is an increasing emphasis on the interior, or the environment itself, which plays a central role in the composition. The first painter of figures who was consistent in this was Pieter de Hooch (1629-after 1684), who worked in Delft until 1660, and then went to Amsterdam. The light and atmosphere in his interiors are essential elements in De Hooch's work. He was probably in contact with Johannes Vermeer (1632-1675) during his years in Delft. Vermeer, the greatest master of paintings of burghers, elevated light itself to become the subject of his paintings. Like no other painter, Vermeer succeeded in capturing reality in the light falling on the figures, which gave the space a visual and expressive character. His concentrated, austere and quiet compositions, usually with only one or two figures, such as *The Lacemaker* or *The Painter's Studio*, reveal a rare, harmonious and subtle use of colour, and a complete control of perspective. In the last work, Vermeer not only concentrated on faithfully representing what he observed, but also produced an allegory on painting. Symbols and reality are thus combined in a masterful way by this brilliant painter of light, who was soon forgotten after his death, and only rediscovered by the Impressionists.

STILL LIFES

The combination of symbols and a faithful representation of the subject is an essential characteristic of seventeenth-century still lifes, which were extremely popular with private collectors in all their forms, although they were not much valued as a genre. It was only the painters of floral arrangements - who actually form a separate genre - who were very well paid. Most painters of still lifes could earn a living only through the sheer quantity of their work. The painters of the "higher genres" looked down on the still life, which was even considered as a subject for "weak minds" by the classicist Gerard de Lairesse. A few hundred Dutch and Flemish painters specialized in the genre, which produced countless masterworks of great technical perfection and virtuosity. The painstaking and tender representation of "still" objects was already striking in the work of the fifteenth-century painter, Jan van Eyck, and the faithful representation of flowers and plants had a tradition which went back to illuminated manuscripts. Towards the end of the sixteenth century, the still life was developed by the painters of Antwerp to become a genre in its own right, and from there it quickly spread to the north.

Flemish artists played an important role in the development of the genre in the Northern Netherlands. For example, the paintings of flowers flourished under the influence of Ambrosius II Bosschaert, who fled to Middelburg at the end of 1500. This city became an important centre for painters of flowers. Flowers traditionally had a symbolic meaning and the rich bouquets could never be considered merely as botanical studies. For example, tulips had not only become costly and fashionable flowers - new varieties were sold for gigantic sums from 1620 - which were depicted in different colours and varieties, but the flowers were often used as a symbol of the transience of life. The symbolic meaning of the bouquets is also apparent from the fact that flowers from different seasons are put together in arrangements. Flies and empty shells are other symbols of transience which were used both by painters of flowers and by still life painters. Even in the work of the last important painter of flowers, who was born just before the end of the Golden Century, the Amsterdam artist, Jan van Huysum (1682-1749), these references can still be discerned.

Another popular subject was the combination of flowers and fruit as in the *Still life with Fruit* by the painter from Utrecht, Jan Davidsz. de Heem (c. 1606-1684), who excelled in so-called "vanitas" still lifes (still lifes in which the symbolism of the transience of life is the central theme). In addition to the Vanitas still lifes and the opulent still lifes which became popular after 1640, portraying glassware, goblets, game, fruit and so on, there was an important category of paintings of "pastry, breakfast and tobacco". This seventeenth century term refers to the modest still lifes which depict food and drink and smoking paraphernalia. From the beginning of the seventeenth century this genre flourished particularly in Haarlem, where painters such as Pieter Claesz. (c. 1597-1661) and Willem Claesz. Heda (1594-1680) produced brilliant and sophisticated works within the restrictions of the subject matter.

Heda died in 1680, the year which can be considered to mark the end of the Golden Century of Dutch painting. The greatest representatives of the Golden Century, such as Frans Hals, Rembrandt, Jan Steen and Vermeer, had died by that year, and the painters who were still alive introduced very few new developments. The waning power of the Republic is also seen as an important factor in the stagnation of innovative movements. However, it is just as probable that painting could not develop further because the achievements of the artists of that century could no longer be surpassed.

Hieronymous Bosch, 1450-1516, The Temptation of St. Anthony, c. 1500
Middle panel of a triptych, 139 x 113 cm
Lisbon, Museu Nacional de Arte Antiga

The significance of the countless details on this panel remains obscure. It does not depict the legends about the temptation of St. Anthony, but a fantastic world of horrors, full of demons, witches and monsters which populate the saint's world when he is tempted.

Lucas van Leyden, 1489/94-1533, The Adoration of the Golden Calf, c. 1525
Middle panel of a triptych, 93 x 67 cm
Amsterdam, Rijksmuseum

Maerten van Heemskerck
1498-1574
Self-portrait, 1553
Panel, 42.2 x 50 cm
Cambridge, Fitzwilliam Museum

One of the most important representatives of Romanism in the northern Netherlands, who depicted himself here against the background of the ruins of the Roman Forum.

Pieter Aertsen, 1509-1575, The Egg Dance, 1557
Panel, 84 x 172 cm, Amsterdam, Rijksmuseum

The best known work by the artist from Amsterdam who was registered in the artists' guild in Antwerp in 1535. Like Pieter Bruegel, he often used village life as a subject.

Pieter Bruegel, 1528/30-1569
The Magpie on the Gallows, 1568
Panel, 45.9 x 50.8 cm
Darmstadt, Hessisches Landesmuseum

Bruegel painted his most lyrical landscape shortly before his death. The symbolism of the stones under the gallows is by no means clear, but the magpie refers to the babbling tongues which Bruegel would send to the gallows. He left the work to his wife in his will.

Cornelis Cornelisz. van Haarlem, 1562-1638
The Wedding of Peleus and Thetis, 1593
Canvas, 246 x 419 cm
Haarlem, Frans Hals Museum

One of the main works by this important mannerist, who had a predilection for biblical and mythological works, with many nudes who moved dynamically. He also painted some works of arquebusiers which were in advance of the genre.

817

Gerard van Honthorst, 1590-1656
Adoration of the Shepherds, 1622
Canvas, 164 x 190 cm
Cologne, Wallraf-Richartz-Museum

Like Terbrugghen, Honthorst spent some time in Italy, and while he was there he painted mainly biblical scenes, like this work. However, after returning to the Netherlands, he started to paint genre works with soldiers, musicians and card players because there was no interest in his religious works.

Hendrick Terbrugghen, 1588-1629, The Flute Player, 1621
Canvas, 70 x 55 cm
Kassel, Staatliche Kunstsammlungen

The most vibrant representative of the school of Utrecht went to Rome for ten years in 1606. After his return he was very successful with compositions of half figures, often playing musical instruments. This type of painting, which Honthorst also did, was based on the work of the Italian, Bartelomeo Manfredi.

ÆTA·SVÆ2
A° 1624·

24

Jan Cornelisz. Verspronck
1597-1662
Girl in Blue, 1641
Canvas, 82 x 66.5 cm
Amsterdam. Rijksmuseum

Verspronck was a gifted portrait painter, and was greatly admired by his contemporaries, though he was less of a virtuoso than Hals. The neutral, often grey background, which contrasts sharply with the outlines of his models, is characteristic of his work.

Frans Hals, 1580/85-1666
The Laughing Cavalier, 1624
Canvas, 86 x 69 cm
London, Wallace Collection

Frans Hals is undoubtedly the most important Dutch portrait painter. His oeuvre consists mainly of portraits and group portraits. This lively painting of a 26-year-old man, executed with enormous virtuosity, reveals his brilliance in this genre.

Rembrandt van Rijn, 1606-1669
The Nightwatch, (The Arquebusiers are preparing to march under Captain
Frans Banning Cocq and Lieutenant Willem van Ruytenburg), 1642
Canvas, 363 x 437 cm
Amsterdam, Rijksmuseum

This painting of the arquebusiers is undoubtedly one of the most famous paintings in the
world. It differs from all the other works in this genre because of the theatrical use of
chiaroscuro and the unusual, disorderly composition, amongst other things.

Rembrandt van Rijn, 1606-1669, Self-portrait, 1640
Canvas, 102 x 80 cm
London, National Gallery

Rembrandt portrays himself as an extremely distinguished character. The canvas is about half the size of that by Titian on which it was based.

Govaert Flinck, 1615-1660
Isaac Blessing Jacob, 1639
Canvas, 117 x 141 cm
Amsterdam, Rijksmuseum

A successful, early biblical work by Flinck which clearly shows the influence of Rembrandt.

Carel Fabritius, 1622-1654
The Beheading of St. John the Baptist
Canvas, 149 x 121 cm
Amsterdam, Rijksmuseum

One of the few works which have survived by this promising pupil of Rembrandt's. Many of his paintings were probably lost in 1654 when there was an enormous explosion of gunpowder which destroyed part of Delft, and Fabritius was killed.

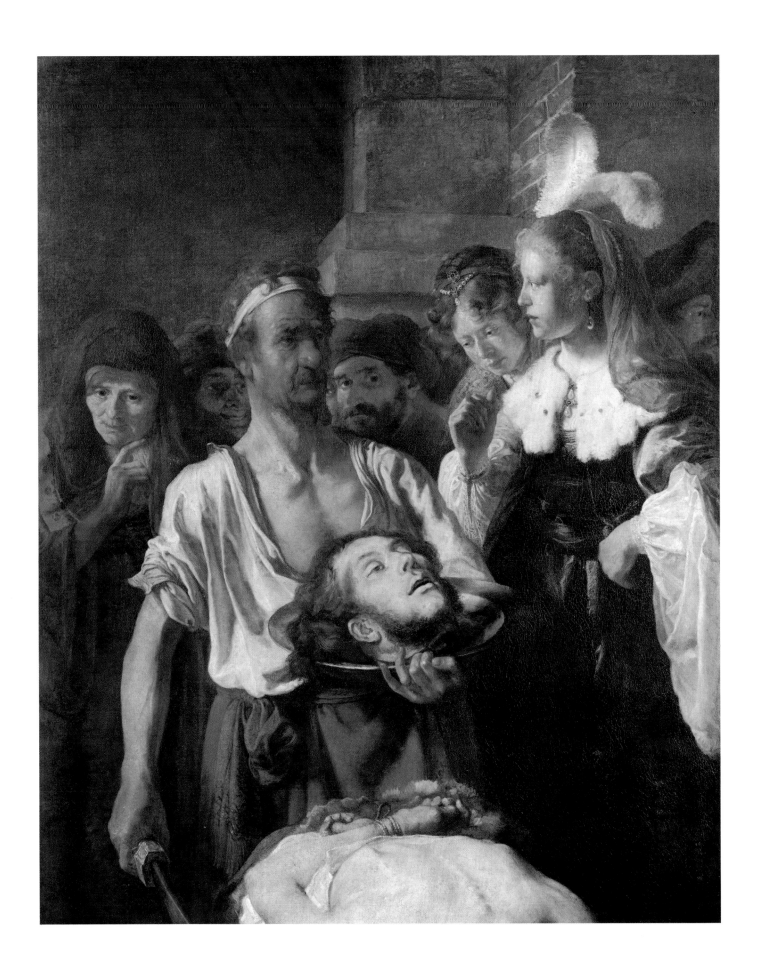

Bartholomeus van der Helst, 1613-1670
The Regents of the Kloveniersdoelen Eating a Meal of Oysters, 1655
Canvas, 171 x 283 cm
Amsterdam, Amsterdams Historisch Museum

The technically perfect, evenly illuminated group portraits by this painter were more popular with his contemporaries than works by Rembrandt, such as "The Nightwatch".

Thomas de Keyser, 1596/97-1667
Constantijn Huygens and his Clerk, 1627
Panel, 92.4 x 69.3 cm
London, National Gallery

This painting of the famous Dutch writer by the son of the architect, Hendrick de Keyser, is a magnificent example of Dutch portraiture.

Hendrick Avercamp, 1585-1634
A Scene on the Ice near a Town, c. 1610
Panel, 58 x 89.8 cm
London, National Gallery

The deaf mute painter from Kampen spent his apprenticeship in Amsterdam, where he was born. Avercamp concentrated virtually exclusively on painting wintry landscapes which were always packed with meticulously represented figures.

Aert van der Neer, 1604-1677
View of the River in Winter
Canvas, 55.5 x 64 cm
Amsterdam, Rijksmuseum

A wintry view by one of the few landscape painters from seventeenth century Amsterdam.
The subtle use of light and colour is characteristic of Van der Neer's work.

Isaak van Ostade, 1621-1649
A Winter Scene with an Inn, c. 1645
Panel, 48.8 x 40 cm
London, National Gallery

Philips Wouwerman, 1619-1668
The White Horse, c. 1640-45
Panel, 43.5 x 38 cm
Amsterdam, Rijksmuseum

Jan van Goyen, 1596-1656, River Landscape, c. 1625
Panel, 40 x 65 cm, Zurich, Kunsthaus, Stiftung Emil G. Bührle

Van Goyen was very important for the development of landscape painting in Holland.

Philips Koninck, 1619-1688, Distant View with Cottages lining a Road, 1655
Canvas, 133 x 167.5 cm, Amsterdam, Rijksmuseum

Koninck was one of the last generation of Dutch landscape painters in the Golden Century. His work was influenced by Rembrandt, and the broad panoramas of water landscapes seen from a fairly high viewpoint are characteristic of his work.

Paulus Potter, 1625-1654, Young Bull, 1647
Canvas, 235.5 x 309 cm, The Hague, Mauritshuis

Potter used cattle as the subject for his famous and popular works. He is considered to be the founder of true animal paintings or "animal landscapes".

Jacob Isaacsz. van Ruisdael, 1628/29-1682
Landscape with the Jewish Cemetery, c. 1665-60
Canvas, 135 x 172.5 cm
Detroit, Institute of Arts

The gravestones which inspired Jacob van Ruisdael can still be seen in the Jewish Cemetery, which survives to this day in Ouderkerk aan de Amstel.
The ruin resembles that of the Abbey in Egmond, but the landscape is painted from the artist's imagination. With his dramatic, monumental interpretations of the landscape, this great landscape painter from the second half of the seventeenth century had a great influence on the Romantic painters a century later.

Salomon van Ruysdael, 1600-1670
Village by the River, 1645
Panel, 64 x 93 cm
Zurich, collection Emil G. Bührle

This early work by Salomon van Ruysdael, the uncle of Jacob Isaacksz., bears a close resemblance to that of Van Goyen, but from 1640 there were drastic changes in his style. The colours became brighter, the clouds contrasted more strongly, and the composition was virtually always dominated by a single group of tall trees. In addition, he also started to paint broad expanses of water, so that the land played only a subordinate role.

Salomon van Ruysdael, 1600-1670
Halt at an Inn, 1648
Panel, 70 x 92 cm
Private collection

Meindert Hobbema, 1638-1709
The Avenue, Middelharnis, c. 1689
Canvas, 103.5 x 141 cm
London, National Gallery

This painting is famous for its strict, geometrical composition, combined with the eccentricities of nature, which counteract all straight lines.
In addition, it is striking that the avenue is the subject of this work, while the town where it leads is an arbitrary feature at the end of the avenue.

Ludolf Backhuysen, 1631-1708
The Y at Amsterdam, Viewed from the Mussel Pier, 1673
Canvas, 81 x 67 cm
Amsterdam, Rijksmuseum

The burgomaster of Amsterdam commissioned this view of Amsterdam as a gift for the Secretary of foreign affairs in Paris, Hugues de Lionne, who owned a collection of paintings of famous cities, though he did not have one of Amsterdam. The painter was paid 1275 guilders for the work.

Jan van de Capelle, 1626-1679
Becalmed, undated
Canvas, 47 x 60 cm
Cologne, Wallraf-Richartz-Museum

The Amsterdam merchant, Van de Capelle, was a singular character. He was self-taught and painted only
for pleasure. Nevertheless, he should be included amongst the great painters of the Golden Century.
Moreover, the wealthy merchant owned an impressive collection of paintings and drawings by leading
artists.
His collection included seven paintings and approximately five hundred drawings by Rembrandt and
ten paintings and four hundred drawings by Jan van Goyen.
The few dated paintings by Jan van de Capelle were done between 1644 and 1663.

Willem van de Velde de Jonge, 1633-1707, The Y at Amsterdam with the "Golden Lion", the former flagship of Cornelis Tromp, 1686, Canvas, 179.5 x 316 cm, Amsterdam, Rijksmuseum

Willem van de Velde de Jonge is undoubtedly the most famous of all the Dutch sea painters. His father did excellent black and white pen and ink drawings, and Willem had his first lessons from him at a young age. When father and son joined the court of Charles II of England in 1674, they often worked together. Willem would "colour in" his father's sketches.

Willem van de Velde de Jonge, 1633-1707
The Gust, c. 1670
Canvas, 77 x 63.5 cm
Amsterdam, Rijksmuseum

Pieter Jansz. Saenredam, 1597-1665
The Old Town Hall in Amsterdam, 1657
Panel, 64.5 x 83 cm
Amsterdam, Rijksmuseum

Saenredam, an artist from Haarlem, has a unique place in Dutch painting, with his extremely meticulous architectural paintings.
He painted mainly church interiors, using detailed sketches drawn in situ, and perspective sketches drawn to size, in his studio. However, he also devoted attention to the exteriors of important buildings. He painted not only the old Town Hall in Amsterdam, but also the Mariaplaats in Utrecht, a beautiful work dating from 1663.

Emanuel de Witte, c. 1617-1692
Interior of a Church, 1668
Canvas, 98.5 x 111.5 cm
Rotterdam, Boymans - van Beuningen Museum

Unlike Saenredam, De Witte often painted interiors from his imagination, or produced combinations from various parts of church interiors. He chose unusual angles, so that the architectural elements are accentuated by the light falling on them in a typically Delftian way.

Gerard Dou, 1613-1675, The Dropsical Woman, 1653
Panel, 83 x 67 cm, Paris, The Louvre

Dou was the most important representative of the so-called "Precise School" in Leiden. He had a predilection for "trompe l'oeil" or deceptive images.

Jan Steen, 1626-1679
The Feast of St. Nicholas, 1665-68
Canvas, 82 x 70.5 cm
Amsterdam, Rijksmuseum

The familiar elements of the feast of St. Nicholas are present in this entertaining family scene by Jan Steen, with a wealth of detail, including a cane for the naughty boy.

Frans van Mieris, 1635-1681
Galant scène, 1658
Panel, 43 x 33 cm
The Hague, Mauritshuis

This type of "galant" (or rather mischievous) genre painting was extremely popular in Holland, and Van Mieris, a painter of the "Precise School", who had been an apprentice of Dou, produced countless of these "conversation pieces".

Gerard ter Borch, 1617-1681
The Letter, c. 1660
Canvas, 79.5 x 68 cm
London, Royal Collection

Ter Borch uses the fall of light in a masterful and subtle way in his elegant portraits and representations of wealthy citizens, as in "The Letter", which does not reveal what is taking place between the three characters.

Gabriël Metsu, 1629-1667
The Sick Child, c. 1660
Canvas, 32.2 x 27.2 cm
Amsterdam, Rijksmuseum

Pieter de Hoogh, 1629-1684, The Courtyard of a House in Delft, 1658
Canvas, 73.5 x 60 cm, London, National Gallery

Johannes Vermeer, 1632-1675, The Painter's Studio, c. 1665-70
Canvas, 120 x 100 cm, Vienna, Kunsthistorisches Museum

In this extremely sophisticated work, Vermeer depicts an allegory on the art of painting. The man seen from the back is not the artist himself, but the personification of the painter in general.

Johannes Vermeer, 1632-1675, The Lacemaker, c. 1664-65
Canvas, 24 x 21 cm, Paris, The Louvre

The incomparably subtle way in which Vermeer works with the effects of light in this austere
painting attracts the viewer's complete attention.

Willem Claesz. Heda, 1594-1680
Still Life with a Gilt Goblet, 1635
Panel, 87 x 113 cm
Amsterdam, Rijksmuseum

The so-called "breakfasts", an example of which is shown above, and the collector's still lifes, were a favourite subject which required great skill and some knowledge of symbolism on the part of the painter. For the uninitiated contemporary viewer, the symbols and the references to vanitas (references to vanity, the transience of life) are difficult to identify.
However, the significance of the caterpillars, butterflies and flies on fruit and leaves in the grandiose collector's still lifes by De Heem is not particularly difficult to guess for any contemporary viewer.

Jan Davidsz. de Heem, c. 1606-1683/84, Still Life with Fruit, 1652
Panel, 41.6 x 35.6 cm, Prague, Národní Galerie

Jan van Huysum, 1682-1749, Hollyhocks and Other Flowers in a Vase, c. 1710
Canvas, 62.1 x 52.3 cm, London, National Gallery